LAND OF THE REED PLAINS

AND

OF THE
REED PLAINS

ANCIENT JAPANESE LYRICS
FROM THE MANYOSHU

translation & commentary
by KENNETH YASUDA

CHARLES E. TUTTLE COMPANY : PUBLISHERS
Rutland, Vermont & Tokyo, Japan

Representatives

For Continental Europe:
BOXERBOOKS, INC., *Zurich*

For the British Isles:
PRENTICE-HALL INTERNATIONAL, INC., *London*

For Australasia:
PAUL FLESCH & CO., PTY. LTD., *Melbourne*

For Canada:
M. G. HURTIG, LTD., *Edmonton*

*Published by the Charles E. Tuttle Company, Inc.
of Rutland, Vermont & Tokyo, Japan
with editorial offices at
Suido 1-chome, 2-6, Bunkyo-ku, Tokyo*

*Library of Congress Catalog Card No. 70-188015
International Standard Book No. 0-8048-1036-2*

Printed in Japan

TABLE OF CONTENTS

BY WAY OF PREFACE

THE *Manyoshu* is the oldest, largest, and greatest anthology of Japanese poetry, one which ranks, especially in the pure quality of its lyricism, among the masterpieces of world literature. Its title has been variously translated as "Collection of Myriad Leaves" or, probably with more accuracy, "Collection for Ten Thousand Ages." It contains over four thousand poems of varying length, arranged in twenty volumes. The precise date of its compilation is not known; probably the collection reached its present form sometime late in the eighth century after having been begun some fifty years earlier and added to from time to time. Thus it coincides in time with the golden age of Chinese poetry, when Li Po and Tu Fu were writing, and with the Beowulf epic.

The collection was left unfinished, and its individual volumes differ greatly in length, character of poems included, periods covered (with much overlapping), and degree of systematization. It evidently drew on various sources, such as an earlier anthology, now lost, called the *Kokashu* (Collection of Ancient Poems), unfortunately without giving any authors' names, as well as private collections made by individuals like Kakinomoto Hitomaro and Takahashi Mushimaro. There are copious though incomplete editorial notes and jottings concerning authors, circumstances of composition, sources used, and anecdotes or legends on which poems are based. In short, when confronting the anthology, its compilers, like its modern commentators, suffered from a common problem: the richness of the materials, their variety, and sheer volume are an inestimably valuable embarrassment.

The earliest date given for a poem in the anthology falls in the reign of Emperor Nintoku (313-99 in traditional chronology), while the latest is 759. Although many are undated, it is safe to say that, with the few earlier exceptions, all the Manyo poems were written in the hundred years before 760. A wide range of society is represented, urban and rural, high and low. Jostling side by side are poems by commoners of the lowest rank and poems by emperors and empresses. Here too are verses by princes and princesses of the blood, scions of the noblest and oldest families, pretenders to the throne, courtesans and courtiers of all ranks, common soldiers, and peasant maids. The subject matter is equally varied, though with a few recurring themes that remain long in the memory—love in all its aspects, from the most spiritual to the frankly sensual; the sorrows of parting and separation; fealty to one's sovereign or lord; longings for home and loved ones; and, always, the beauties of nature.

The songs of the frontier guards (*sakimori no uta*), who were recruited from various provinces in the east and sent on the long and perilous journey to the southern island of Kyushu to garrison Japanese outposts against possible invasions from Korea, or to the north to take part in the continuous struggles with the aborigines, express the anguish of partings and longing for home, as also do the laments of high commanders at Dazaifu, the headquarters of the Kyushu defenses. The "songs of the Eastland" (*Azuma-uta*) derived from the Kanto region, which today includes Tokyo and was then a pioneer frontier far removed from the luxuries of the capital. They are characterized by the use of dialect, a certain attractive rusticity of tone, and a peculiar, light rhythm. Sentiments in them tend to be direct and unvarnished, sometimes even bawdy, and the images are homely and related to work. Both these groups of poems are extraordinarily interesting for their apparent authenticity in presenting the voices of the lowly folk.

The pulsing variety of national life is fascinatingly alive throughout the anthology. The scope of the stage, cast of characters, and multiplicity of entangle-ments create a richly generous depth to this ancient period, giving it an actuality and immediacy which favor very few eras of the distant past.

In the early Manyo period, the Imperial court was in Yamato, centering about present-day Kyoto and Osaka, and carried on a fairly lively intercourse with the ancient Korean kingdom of Paikche, which in 405 sent a learned man, one Wani, to Japan. His appearance at the Japanese court marks the official adoption of the Chinese written language by Japan, which had had no writing of its own. Aside from this momentous event, intercourse with Paikche re-sulted also in the introduction of Buddhism to Japan in the middle of the sixth century. From this point on, the cultural impetus of contact with the supe-rior civilization of China, known first through Korea and later directly from China itself, was accelerated, reaching one climax in the founding of Nara in 710 as the new seat of the Imperial court and the center of Buddhist teachings.

Along with these foreign influences, the national leaders were preoccupied with the constant attempt to bring political order and stability to the country by a strengthening of the central government at the expense of the clans and the conquest of outlying rebellious groups as well as the Ainu in the north-east. The rise and fall of the great families surrounding the throne is a constant motif also, beginning with the Soga in the sixth century, the Otomo, and the final ascendancy of the Fujiwara.

It was a fascinating time, this Manyo age, and a most formative historical period. A fuller background is painted in the introduction to that excellent work of the Japanese Classics Translation Committee, *The Manyoshu: One Thousand Poems Selected and Translated from the Japanese* (Iwanami, Tokyo, 1940), now badly needing to be brought back into print.

The great names of this storied past found in the *Manyoshu* seem to rustle the very skirts of history herself. The fancy of the fabulously cruel Emperor Yuraku (418-79), one of whose milder sports was the shooting of men from trees for target practice, is taken with a pretty country lass carrying a trowel and basket. The benevolent patron of Buddhism Prince Shotoku (574-622), whose humane exhortations to his country in his celebrated constitution are justly revered, laments the death of some anonymous traveler whose body he sees by a mountain roadside. Fujiwara Kamatari (614-69), founder of the Fujiwara fortunes and descendant of a family coeval with the Imperial line, whose political sagacity and shrewdness rid the court of the arrogant Soga tyrants in one lightning coup, is jubilant over his winning of the court maiden Yasumiko. Emperor Shomu (701-56), whose pious widow, by depositing his personal effects in the treasure-house of the Shoso-in, has delighted generations of scholars, archeologists, and artists, bids a gracious and imperial farewell to his royal inspectors as they set out for the distant provinces.

Here too are the magic names of some of Japan's most renowned poets: the two "saints of poetry" Hitomaro and Akahito, the lyrical Yakamochi and his father Tabito, philosophical Okura, homesick Kurohito, and legend-loving Mushimaro. And the poetesses: the flirtatious Princess Nukada, Chief Priestess Princess Oku, and tragic Sanu Chigami, who married above her station.

But a great number of the poems, including some of the most notable, are by men and women so little known that in some cases nothing remains but their names and, in other cases, not even that. This is particularly true of the songs of the frontier guards and the "Eastland songs." It is precisely these verses by unknown singers that give such substance and credibility to the Manyo world, communicating across the stretch of twelve hundred years, across the abysm of differences in cultural sensibilities, across, it is hoped, the hazards of translation. When the Japanese speak of the Manyo world, they conjure up a vision washed by a purer, cleaner, more heroic air than has been, they feel, a part of their history since. There is preserved also in this collection a quality which is, they feel, completely Japanese, contrasting with the Chinese-style writing that began its first great vogue about the same time and probably accounts for the *Manyoshu*'s having been left unfinished—a quality that never again occurs in Japanese literature with quite this degree of purity.

More than ninety percent of the poems are in the *tanka* form, which consists of thirty-one syllables arranged in five lines of 5-7-5-7-7 syllables. This is still a dominant verse form today: all poems submitted in the annual Imperial poetry contest, which in 1959 attracted more than 23,000 entrants, are *tanka*. Examples of a longer form known as *choka*, in which lines of five and seven syllables alternate to any length and terminate with a seven-syllable line, are found also, including several masterpieces by Hitomaro. To a *choka* are usually attached several envoys, usually in the *tanka* form. Other minor and now obsolete forms also appear in the anthology.

The historical periods covered by the *Manyoshu*, as conventionally given, are:

> Pre-Omi—prior to 667
> Omi—667-73
> Asuka—673-86
> Fujiwara—686-710
> Nara—710-84.

* * *

The order of these poems aims, roughly, at emphasizing the three great geographical and, to a lesser degree, social divisions of the Manyo world: the Yamato heartland (pages 17-83), the Kyushu of the frontier guards (pages 84-94), and the "Eastland" of the pioneers (pages 95-116). My translations have been made from the critical texts given by Dr. Yukichi Takeda in his *Zotei Manyoshu Zenchushaku*, to which I have added my own notes and comments. The standard volume and poem numbers are shown in brackets at the end of each note. I have tried to make my translations as literal as the exigencies of transforming verse from Japanese to English allow, occasionally with some slight addition in the interest of making a poem reasonably understandable without need of a lengthy gloss. My standards of rendering Japanese verse into English have already been set forth in my book *The Japanese Haiku* (Tuttle, 1957) and need not be repeated here beyond pointing out that I follow the same syllable patterns of the originals.

KENNETH YASUDA

Tokyo

LAND OF THE REED PLAINS

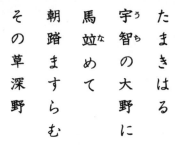

たまきはる

宇智の大野に

馬竝めて

朝踏ますらむ

その草深野

THROUGH wide Uchi Plain
with the horses drawn abreast
this early morning
I think he must be riding ...
through that thickly grass-grown field.

*Ascribed to Empress Kogyoku (594-661). An envoy
to a poem sent her husband, Emperor Jomei, in 641
on the occasion of a hunting expedition he made on
the Uchi Plain.* [1:4]

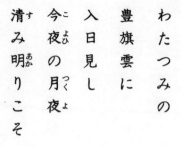

わたつみの
豊旗雲に
入日見し
今夜の月夜
清み明りこそ

ON the clouds that trail
like richly colored banners
far across the sea,
the setting sun is shining . . .
clear must be the moon tonight.

By Emperor Tenji (613-71), while still Crown Prince.
Shown as the second envoy to a poem based on a legend
of three quarreling mountains, but probably intended
as an independent poem. [1 : 15]

18

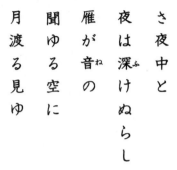

さ夜中と
夜は深けぬらし
雁が音ねの
聞ゆる空に
月渡る見ゆ

THE hour advances
far into the heart of night;
across the heavens,
where the geese are heard in flight,
I see the moon go sailing.

From the "Hitomaro Collection." The authorship of the poems in this group has not been clearly established although many are undoubtedly by Kakinomoto Hitomaro, an official of low rank in the Fujiwara period. He is the greatest Manyo poet, known to posterity as a "saint of poetry." This much-admired poem is a characteristically direct statement without art or manipulation—strong, bare, and inevitable. [9 : 1701]

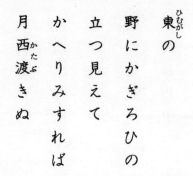

東の
野にかぎろひの
立つ見えて
かへりみすれば
月西渡きぬ

On eastern meadows
glows the rosy tint of dawn
with a faint, soft gleam;
and as I glance behind me
there the moon is sinking low.

By Hitomaro. An envoy to a long poem composed in 767, one of the greatest in the Manyoshu. [1 : 48]

20

引馬野に
にほふ榛原
入り乱れ
衣にほはせ
旅の験に

IN Hikuma Field
bloom the lespedeza flowers;
so pass among them
and in token of your tour
tint your robes in fragrant hues.

By Naga Okimaro. On the occasion of an imperial progress made by the retired Empress Jito to Mikawa Province in 702 [1 : 57]

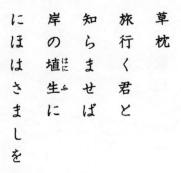

HOW I wish I had known
beforehand of this journey
you would make, my lord:
with the red clay from the banks
I would have dyed a robe for you!

By "a girl of Suminoe." Presented to Prince Naga,
presumably the fourth son of Emperor Temmu, in
699. There is evidence that the girl was of quite low
rank, perhaps the commonest of commoners, though the
words show great intimacy.   [1 : 69]

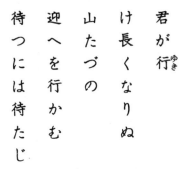

君が行き
け長くなりぬ
山たづの
迎へを行かむ
待つには待たじ

O BELOVED one,
since you went away from me
many days have passed.
I must go and search for you,
for I cannot wait alone.

*By Empress Iwa-no-Hime (d. 347), official consort of
the benevolent Emperor Nintoku. This is one of four
poems of longing for her absent husband, which are
among the oldest in the* Manyoshu. [2 : 90]

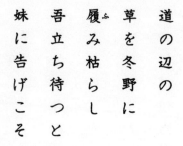

道の辺の
草を冬野に
履み枯らし
吾立ち待つと
妹に告げこそ

TELL the one I love
that I stand and long for her,
stamping on the grass
by the roadside till it turns
withered gray like winter fields.

From the Kokashu. *This poem describes one of the rare occasions when the waiting lover is the man rather than the woman.*   [11 : 2776]

24

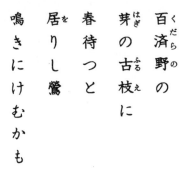

百済野の
芽の古枝に
春待つと
居り鶯
鳴きにけむかも

IN Kudara Field
upon the withered branches
of lespedeza,
waiting long for spring to come,
has the uguisu sung?

*By Yamabe Akahito (d. 736?). Together with Hito-
maro, he is known as a "saint of poetry." His forte
was nature poems in a limpid, graceful strain. The
uguisu, commonly rendered as "nightingale," is Japan's
most melodious songbird.* [8 : 1431]

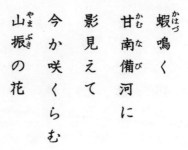

蝦鳴く
甘南備河に
影見えて
今か咲くらむ
山振の花

THE yellow roses
will be blooming soon again,
their blossoms mirrored
on the Kamunabi Stream
where the frogs are singing now.

By Prince Atsumi (late Nara period). The call of the Japanese frog, unlike the croaking of its Western counterpart, is considered sweet and melodious. [8 : 1435]

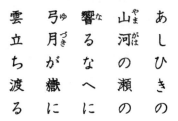

THE rushing rapids
of the mountain river roar,
while across the peak
of lofty Mt. Yutsuki
the clouds ascend and hover.

*By Hitomaro. Here is the tone of loftiness, vigor, and
grand seriousness associated with Hitomaro's work.*

[7 : 1088]

丈夫の
鞆の音すなり
もののふの
大臣
楯立つらしも

WE can hear the sounds
of the warriors' elbow-guards:
the lord general
of the military clans
must be ranging battle shields.

*By Empress Gemmyo (661–721). Composed in 708,
the poem refers perhaps to preparations for the expedi-
tionary force sent against the aboriginal Ainu in 709.
The sound referred to is the snapping of bow strings
against the guards worn on the left arm to protect it
from the snapback.* [1 : 76]

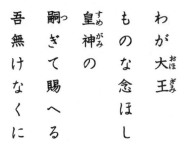

わが大王 おほぎみ
ものな念ほし
皇神 すめがみ の
嗣っぎて賜へる
吾無けなくに

O MIGHTY sovereign,
be not concerned so deeply
sent as closest kin
by our sacred deities,
am I not here to aid you?

*By Princess Minabe, elder sister of Empress Gemmyo.
Composed in 708, this is a reply to the preceding
poem.*   [1 : 77]

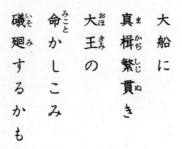

大船に
真楫繁貫き
大王の
命かしこみ
礒廻するかも

IN awed obedience
to our Majesty's command,
in his mighty ship,
full-oared on either gunwale,
all along the coasts we go.

By Isonokami (Lord of Iso). According to the original
Manyo note, the author might be Isonokami Otomaro
(d. 750), one time governor of Echizen.   [3 : 368]

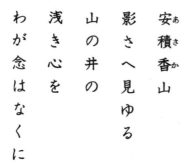

安積香山
影さへ見ゆる
山の井の
浅き心を
わが念はなくに

WITH Asaka Hill
reflected on the water
clearly from afar,
shallow lies the mountain spring;
but no shallow heart is mine.

*By "a former lady in waiting." An extempore poem
recited before Prince Katsuraki (Tachibana Moroe,
684–757) to assuage his anger because of the meager
reception accorded him by a provincial governor and to
assure him of the assembled company's respect and
loyalty. The effect is based both upon the shallowness
of the pool and a word-play between Asaka Hill and
shallow (asaki) heart.* [16 : 3807]

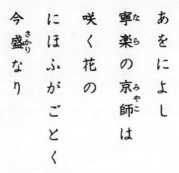

あをによし
寧楽（なら）の京師（みやこ）は
咲く花の
にほふがごとく
今盛（さかり）なり

OH, our capital,
this green-delightful Nara,
is in glory now
and at the height of beauty,
like flowers in fragrant bloom!

*By Ono Oyu (d. 737). The best of the poems on Nara,
this embodies to a high degree the vaunted Manyo
quality: direct, spontaneous lyricism, refined but sturdy
and with no preciosity.* [3 : 328]

春の苑その
紅くれないにほふ
桃の花
下した照る道に
出で立つ嬢をとめ

IN the spring garden
how crimson, rich, and fragrant
glow the peach blossoms—
and in the flower-lit lane
beneath, a maiden walking!

By Otomo Yakamochi (718-85), member of an ancient, powerful clan, a brilliant poet, and the last of the compilers of the Manyoshu *itself. His work sweeps with authority and an unmistakable personal stamp over a wide range of subjects. This is one of two poems composed the evening of March 1, 750; gaily brilliant and sensuous, it is one of the well-known poems of the collection.* [19 : 4139]

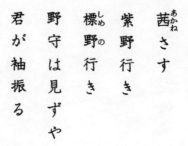

茜さす
紫野行き
標野の行き
野守は見ずや
君が袖振る

GOING back and forth
through the scarlet, purple lea,
through the roped-off field,
would the guardsman notice you?
Oh, you wave your sleeve at me!

By Princess Nukada, the greatest poetess of her time. She was the favorite of Emperor Tenji, whom she accompanied on a hunting expedition on May 5, 668, the occasion of this poem. It was addressed to the emperor's brother, which explains the note of caution. The brother eventually succeeded to the throne, becoming Emperor Temmu and father of Princess Nukada's daughter. The poetess must have been a person of magnetism as well as talent. [1 : 20]

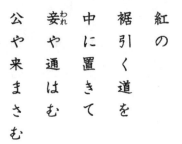

紅の
裾引く道を
中に置きて
妾や通はむ
公や来まさむ

BRIGHT and crimson red,
my robes trail along the path
that leads between us. . . .
Shall I follow it to you?
Won't you follow it to me?

Apparently from the Kokashu.   [11 : 2655]

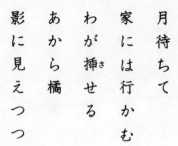

月待ちて
家には行かむ
わが挿せる
あから橘
影に見えつつ

I SHALL wait a while,
for the moon to rise and shine,
and then start homeward
when the red mandarin-flowers
in my hair cast a shadow.

By Princess Awata (d. 764). An extempore poem composed at a banquet given by Lord Tachibana Moroe in 744. The mandarin too is called tachibana. *Poetic wit of this type was much appreciated.* [18 : 4060]

丈夫と
思へるものを
刀佩きて
かにはの田井に
芹子ぞ採みける

THOUGH I thought of you
as a gallant warrior,
did you gird your sword
just to gather water-cress
in the Kaniha rice fields?

By "Myokan." Sent to Lord Tachibana Moroe around
740 in playful acknowledgement of a gift of water-
cress.   [20 : 4456]

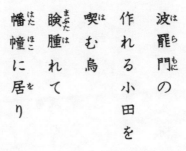

波羅門の
作れる小田を
喫む烏
瞼腫れて
幡幢に居り

WITH swollen eyelids,
upon the lance-head streamer
sits a crow that fed
greedily on the paddy field
tended by the Brahmin priest!

*By Prince Takamiya (middle Nara period). Perhaps
the priest referred to is the Indian who, it is recorded,
came to Japan by way of China in 736. The crow
here is punished for stealing sacred property. Streamers
attached to lances were set up in temple compounds on
days of special note.* [16 : 3856]

38

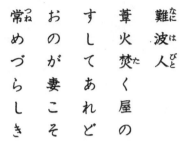

難波人
葦火焚く屋の
すしてあれど
おのが妻こそ
常めづらしき

THOUGH my wife grows old
and as soot-black as the huts
where Naniwa folk
make their fires of river-reeds,
always fresh she seems to me.

From the Kokashu. *The gay homeliness of the image
suggests a folk origin. River-reeds were used as fuel
by the poorer classes. Naniwa was a small port where
the city of Osaka is now located.* [11 : 2651]

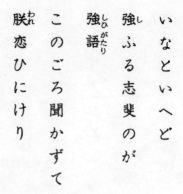

いなといへど
強《し》ふる志斐のが
強語《しひがたり》
このごろ聞かずて
朕《われ》恋ひにけり

THOUGH I said, "No more!"
how that Shihi would persist
in telling her tales!
Now, not seeing her of late,
I sigh and yearn to hear them.

By Empress Jito (645-702), official consort of and successor to Emperor Temmu. Nothing is known of the garrulous Lady Shihi except her playfully indignant reply to the empress's poem, which follows. [3 : 236]

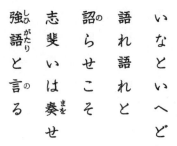

いなといへど
語れ語れと
詔の らせこそ
志斐いは奏せ
強語と言る

THOUGH I said, "No more!"
how you always urged me on
to yet another!
And now it is you who say,
"How that Shihi would persist!"

By "Lady Shihi," in reply to the preceding poem.
[3 : 237]

御民吾
生ける験_{しるし}あり
天地の
栄ゆる時に
遇_あへらく念へば

AT the very thought
that earth and heaven prosper
I, your subject, feel
this life of ours worth living:
in your glorious age we dwell.

*By Ama no Inukai Okamaro. Composed in 734, per-
haps at a New Year's celebration held by Emperor
Shomu, this is considered the most memorable of the
Manyo poems in praise of sovereigns.* [6 : 996]

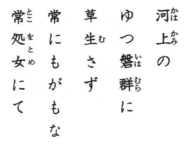

河上の
ゆつ磐群に
草生さず
常にもがもな
常処女にて

JUST as no grass grows
on those countless craggy rocks
in the upper stream,
forever so a maiden
may our royal princess be.

*By Lady Fuki. Written on the way to worship the Sun
Goddess at Ise Shrine in February, 675, at first reading this is a pious wish that her mistress, Princess
Toöchi (d. 678), remain eternally young. There are
probably other interpretations, since it had been the
unhappy lot of this princess, the daughter of Princess
Nukada and Emperor Temmu (see p. 34), to see her
father defeat her husband, Emperor Kobun (d. 672),
in a succession war.* [1 : 22]

海行かば
水浸く屍
山行かば
草むす屍
大皇の
辺にこそ死なめ
顧みは為じ

IF we go by sea,
salt-soaked be my body;
if we go by land,
grass-covered be my body:
let me gladly die
by our mighty sovereign's side,
never, never falling back.

By Yakamochi. A stanza from a poem celebrating the discovery of gold, in 749, which made possible the completion of the great Buddha of Nara. Here, with the introductory line "We are the sons of the fathers who sang [the following]," the poet-warrior celebrates the long history of his clan's loyalty to the Imperial line. The passage appears to be part of an Otomo clan song, or at least a close paraphrase. [18 : 4094]

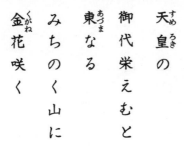

天皇の<ruby>天<rt>すめ</rt></ruby><ruby>皇<rt>ろき</rt></ruby>の
御代栄えむと
<ruby>東<rt>あづま</rt></ruby>なる
みちのく山に
<ruby>金<rt>くがね</rt></ruby>花咲く

As a sign that tells
how our sovereign's reign shall prosper,
in the Eastern Land,
in the Michinoku mountains,
gold has blossomed into flower.

By Yakamochi. One of three envoys to the congratu-
latory poem discussed on the preceding page.

[18 : 4097]

石灑ぐ
垂水の上の
さ蕨の
萌え出づる春に
なりにけるかも

ABOVE the water
gliding softly down the rocks,
the buds of bracken
burgeoning in tender green—
spring has come already!

By Prince Shiki (Fujiwara period). It is not known which of two imperial princes bearing this name was the poet. This verse is one of the greatest written on early spring, that ineffable first flush where the green is hardly more than a delicate haze. [8 : 1418]

46

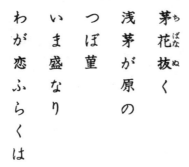

茅花抜く
浅茅が原の
つぼ菫
いま盛なり
わが恋ふらくは

IN miscanthus fields
where we plucked the reed's young ears,
now the violets
are blooming in their glory;
so my longing grows for you.

*By "the elder daughter of Lady Otomo of Tamura"
(late Nara period). Sent to her younger half-sister,
the wife of Yakamochi.* [8 : 1449]

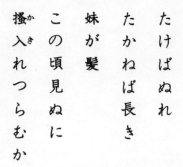

たけばぬれ
たかねば長き
妹が髪
この頃見ぬに
掻か入きれつらむか

DOWN your hair would slip
even if bound tight; untied,
it was much too long.
Do you tuck it up these days
while I cannot see you yet?

By Mikata Shami (late Fujiwara period?). Sent to his wife during the author's illness, shortly after their marriage. See her reply on the next page. In Manyo times husbands and wives of the aristocratic classes maintained separate households. [2 : 123]

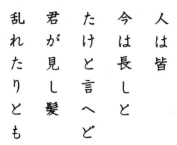

人は皆
今は長しと
たけと言へど
君が見し髪
乱れたりとも

THOUGH now everyone
tells me I should bind my hair
for it's grown too long,
I keep it as you saw it,
however tangled it becomes.

By the wife of Mikata Shami, in answer to the preceding poem.   [2:124]

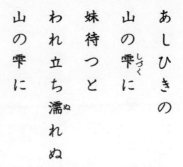

あしひきの
山の雫に
妹待つと
われ立ち濡れぬ
山の雫に

IN the drops of dew
at the sloping mountain base
waiting for my love,
I stood and I was drenched
with the drops of mountain dew.

By Prince Otsu (663-86). One of the many sons of Emperor Temmu, he was killed in the succession dispute following his father's death and is remembered as an accomplished scholar and poet in both Japanese and Chinese. This and the following poem were exchanged sometime before 685. [2 : 107]

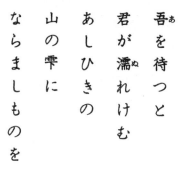

WAITING long for me
at the sloping mountain base
you were soaked, my lord,
with the drops of mountain dew:
how I wish that I were they!

By "Lady Ishikawa," in reply to the preceding poem.
[2 : 108]

51

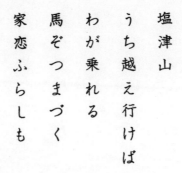

塩津山
うち越え行けば
わが乗れる
馬ぞつまづく
家恋ふらしも

PAST Mt. Shiotsu
the horse that I am riding
has tripped and staggered;
so I know the one at home
must be longing after me.

By Kasa Kanamura (early Nara period), a nobleman
and member of a family of poets.   [3 : 365]

夕されば
小倉の山に
鳴く鹿は
今夜は鳴かず
寝宿にけらしも

W HEN evening comes
on the hill of Ogura,
the deer sounds its call,
but tonight it does not cry...
perhaps it has gone to sleep.

*By Emperor Jomei (593-641). Classified as an autumn
poem in the* Manyoshu; *even in modern poetry the
call of the deer is an autumnal theme. No melancholy
is intended; rather, the poet conveys the rich silence of
a calm autumn evening.* [8 : 1511]

暁と
夜烏鳴けど
この山の上は
木末の上は
いまだ静けし

NIGHT crows are cawing,
telling of the coming dawn;
yet still the treetops
on this peak I cross alone
are deeply hushed in silence.

From the Kokashu. *Thought to have been written by
a man returning home from a love tryst.* [7 : 1263]

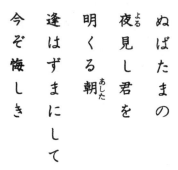

ぬばたまの
夜(よる)見し君を
明くる朝(あした)
逢はずまにして
今ぞ悔しき

MEETING you that night
within the jet-black darkness,
but parting at dawn
without seeing you again—
oh, how I now regret it!

By Sanu Chigami (middle Nara period). One of sixty-three poems exchanged between the poetess and her husband, Nakatomi Yakamori, during his exile, probably between 739 and 741. Tradition has it that she was a very low-ranking employee of a government bureau, while he was a nobleman, and that his exile was because he had clandestinely married beneath him. Her poems are much admired for their directness of feeling and passion. [15 : 3769]

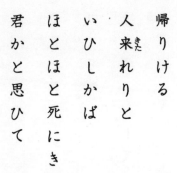

THERE was a person
who had just returned, they said,
and as I listened,
oh, I felt as though I'd die
with the hope it might be you!

By Sanu Chigami (see p. 55). There was an amnesty in 740 and several exiles returned to the capital; her husband, however, had been specifically excluded from the amnesty. [15:3772]

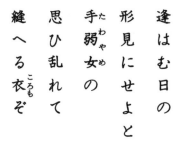

逢はむ日の
形見にせよと
手弱女の
思ひ乱れて
縫へる衣ぞ

THESE are the garments
I, a helpless woman, sewed
with troubled longings
as a token of the day
when we two shall meet again.

By Sanu Chigami (see pp. 55-56). Perhaps attached to some clothes sent her husband in exile.

[15 : 3753]

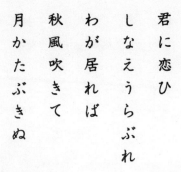

君に恋ひ
しなえうらぶれ
わが居れば
秋風吹きて
月かたぶきぬ

WHILE I stay alone,
feeling weary and forlorn,
longing after you,
the autumn breeze comes blowing,
and the moon sinks to the west.

Apparently from the Kokashu.   [10 : 2298]

58

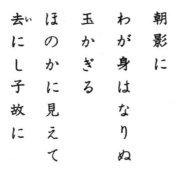

朝影に
わが身はなりぬ
玉かぎる
ほのかに見えて
去にし子故に

AH, like a shadow
cast long by the morning sun,
thin grows my body
for the lovely pearl-like one
who has faintly gone away.

From the "Hitomaro Collection."   [11 : 2394]

59

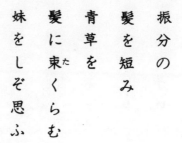

振分の
髪を短み
青草を
髪に束くらむ
妹をしぞ思ふ

HOW I do recall
the girl with her parted hair
hanging shoulder-long!...
Thinking it still much too short,
she had bound it long with grass.

From the Kokashu. A girl's short hair was allowed to lengthen as she approached marriageable age. The impatient young woman here attempts to lengthen her hair with long blades of grass so she can put it up.

[11 : 2540]

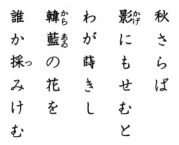

秋さらば
影にもせむと
わが蒔きし
韓藍の花を
誰か採みけむ

OH, that in autumn
I might have some dye, I thought,
when I sowed the seeds
of the lovely cockscomb plant—
but who has plucked its blossom?

Apparently from the Kokashu. *Here the lament of love's labor lost is given piquancy by the mention of the cockscomb.* [7 : 1362]

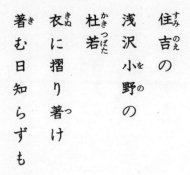

住吉の
浅沢小野の
杜若
衣に摺り着け
著む日知らずも

THE flags are blooming
in Asazawa Meadow
at Suminoe,
but I do not know what day
I shall wear the silk she dyes.

Apparently from the Kokashu. An exchange of garments was often part of the marriage ritual.

[7:1361]

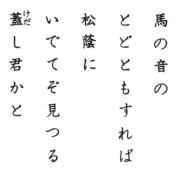

馬の音の
とどともすれば
松蔭に
いでてぞ見つる
蓋(けだ)し君かと

EACH time when I hear
the sounding of horses' hoofs,
out I go and look,
standing by the shady pines,
with the hope it may be you.

Apparently from the Kokashu.   [11 : 2653]

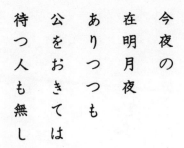

今夜の
在明月夜
ありつつも
公をおきては
待つ人も無し

LIKE the moon tonight,
which will linger on till dawn,
I too will linger. . . .
For no other one but you
would I wait so longingly.

Apparently from the Kokashu.   [11 : 2671]

夕卜にも
占にも告れる
今夜だに
来まさぬ君を
何時とか待たむ

BY vesper augurs
and upon the fortune-sticks
it was clearly told;
but you have not come tonight.
Now when shall I wait for you?

Apparently from the Kokashu. *Many methods of for-
tunetelling were widespread; yuke (evening fortunetell-
ing) is mentioned nine times in the* Manyoshu.

[11 : 2613]

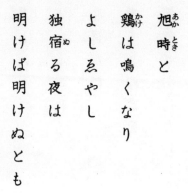

旭時と
鶏は鳴くなり
よしゑやし
独宿る夜は
明けば明けぬとも

THE cock is crowing,
telling of the break of day.
What does it matter
if this night I spend alone
is ending? . . . Then let it end!

Apparently from the Kokashu. *A variation on the
frequent theme of lovers lamenting that they must part
at dawn*   [11 : 2800]

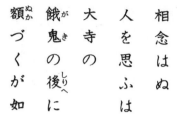

相念はぬ
人を思ふは
大寺の
餓鬼の後に
額づくが如

To long after you
who do not return my love
is like bowing low
to some famished demon's back
before a mighty temple.

*By Lady Kasa (late Nara period), probably a clans-
man of Kasa Kanamaru. One of twenty-four love
poems she sent Yakamochi. The "famished demon"
was probably an image set up as a warning of the
damnation awaiting evil-doers: to address prayers to it
would be patently useless. The poetic figure here is
strangely eccentric for the period, but all Lady Kasa's
verses, as befitting their recipient, show a sophistication
of diction and a new tone.* [4 : 608]

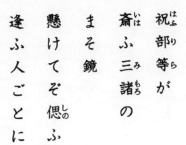

祝部等が
斎ふ三諸の
まそ鏡
懸けてぞ偲ふ
逢ふ人ごとに

LIKE the priest who serves
the shrine and keeps the mirror,
deep within my heart
you I keep, and long for you
each time I meet another.

*Apparently from the Kokashu. The sacred mirror
forms part of the regalia of all Shinto shrines, being
a symbol of the Sun Goddess, the central figure of the
Shinto pantheon.* [12 : 2981]

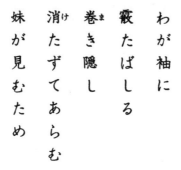

わが袖に
霰たばしる
巻き隠し
消たずてあらむ
妹が見むため

OH, upon my sleeves
the hailstones come scattering!
I would wrap them up
to keep the hail from melting,
and then show them to my love.

Apparently from the Kokashu. [10 : 2312]

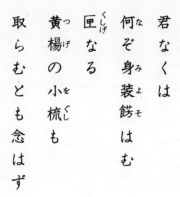

君なくは
何ぞ身装飾はむ
匣なる
黄楊の小梳も
取らむとも念はず

IF you go away,
why should I adorn myself?
From my toilet-case
I shall not think of taking
even my comb of boxwood.

*By "a young woman of Harima." Addressed to an
official as he left to assume a new post in the capital
sometime between 715 and 719. Boxwood combs are
highly valued even today.*   [9 : 1777]

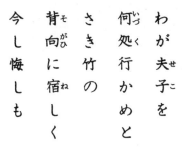

わが夫子を
何処行かめと
さき竹の
背向に宿しく
今し悔しも

SINCE I thought my love
would never depart from me,
back to back we slept
like a bamboo split in two.
How I do regret it now!

Apparently from the Kokashu. *An elegy. Its forthright statement places it among the early Manyo poems, perhaps during the late Fujiwara or early Nara period.*

[7 : 1412]

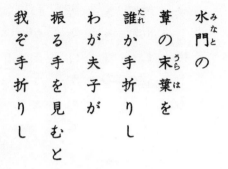

水門の
葦の末葉を
誰か手折りし
わが夫子が
振る手を見むと
我ぞ手折りし

WHO is it that breaks
the tips from the river-reeds
growing by the water-gate?
Wanting still to see
the hand my love is waving,
it is I who breaks them off.

*From the "Hitomaro Collection." This is an example
of the sedoka form, which was already rare by the
time of the Manyoshu and disappeared thereafter. It
consists of two units, each with lines of five, seven, and
seven syllables.*   [7 : 1288]

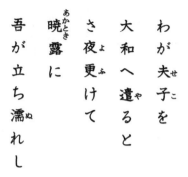

わが夫子を
大和へ遣ると
さ夜更けて
暁露に
吾が立ち濡れし

BIDDING you farewell
as you left for Yamato,
through the deepening night
I stood watching, and was drenched
in the dewdrops of the dawn.

*By Princess Oku (661-701), one of Emperor Temmu's
numerous daughters, who served from the age of four-
teen as the Chief Priestess of Ise Shrine. One of two
poems composed, perhaps in 685, after a secret visit
from her ill-fated brother Prince Otsu, whose early
death (see p. 50) fulfilled her gloomy sentiments.*

[2 : 105]

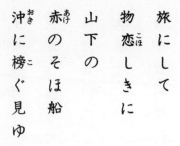

旅にして
物恋しきに
山下の
赤のそほ船
沖に榜ぐ見ゆ

I JOURNEY onward,
beset with homeward longings . . .
And in the offing
there the crimson-painted ship
goes rowing for the open sea.

*By Takechi Kurohito (Fujiwara period), an official
under Empress Jito and her grandson Emperor
Mommu. His duties took him on many journeys away
from the capital, inspiring several excellent travel
poems. Imperial ships were painted red, and here the
sight of one of them bound for the capital increases
his homesickness.* [3 : 270]

74

丈夫の
得物矢手挿み
立ち向ひ
射る円形は
見るに清けし

FOR a warrior
with the arrow to his bow,
carefully aiming—
how clearly this Target Bay,
Matokata, lies in view.

*By "attendant maiden Toneri." The first three lines,
modifying Target Bay, constitute a special poetic device
known as a joshi, a long introductory phrase preceding
the main statement of a poem; its skillful use can
afford sudden surprise and be most legitimate poeti-
cally. Here the point is the statement on the beauty
of a day so clear and sunny that Matokata Bay can
be seen distinctly. "Matokata" can be translated as
"target bay"; hence the first three lines.* [1 : 61]

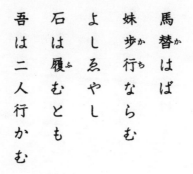

馬替かば
妹歩か行ちならむ
よしゑやし
石は履ふむとも
吾は二人行かむ

AND should I trade
your mirror for a horse, still
you would be afoot;
no, though stepping over rocks,
I would rather walk with you.

Anonymous. The concluding tanka of a set of four poems in the form of a dialogue between a husband and wife who are traveling afoot. In the first three the wife laments that her husband must travel thus and begs him to get himself a horse by trading away her polished metal mirror, a treasured possession in those days, one she had inherited from her mother.

[13 : 3317]

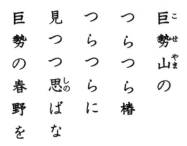

巨勢山の
つらつら椿
つらつらに
見つつ思ばな
巨勢の春野を

THEN, on Kose Hill
row on row camellias bloomed. . . .
Looking once again,
let us fondly now recall
those fair spring fields of Kose.

By Sakato Hitotari. Dated September 18, 701. This poem, on the theme of autumn thoughts of spring, is distinguished in Japanese by its onomatopoetic beauty and by the ancient flavor of its repetitions. [1 : 54]

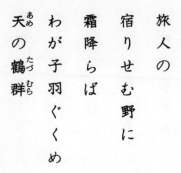

旅人の
宿りせむ野に
霜降らば
わが子羽ぐくめ
天の鶴群

WHEN the frost lies white
upon fields where travelers
must find their shelter,
O flock of heavenly cranes,
cover my child with your wings!

Anonymous. The envoy to a poem addressed by a mother to her son as he departed with an embassy to China in 733. [9 : 1791]

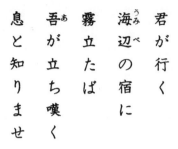

君が行く

海辺の宿に

霧立たば

吾が立ち嘆く

息と知りませ

As you travel on,
if the mist arises white
along the seashore
by your shelter, think of it
as a sigh I breathe at home.

*Anonymous. One of a series of poems written in 736
on the occasion of a departure of an embassy to the
ancient Korean kingdom of Silla.* [15 : 3580]

零<ruby>る<rt>ふ</rt></ruby>雪は
あはにな降りそ
吉隠の<ruby>よなばり</ruby>
猪養の岡の<ruby>るかひ</ruby>
寒かろまくに

O DRIFTING snowflakes,
do not fall so thick and fast;
at Yonabari
on the hill of Igari
it must be cold and chill.

By Prince Hozumi (d. 715), the fifth son of Emperor Temmu, who served as acting prime minister the last ten years of his life. Written in the winter of 708, the poem is an elegy to his half-sister, Princess Tajima, who had died in the summer of that year and been buried on Igari Hill. [2 : 203]

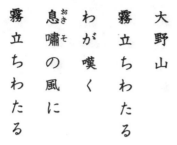

大野山
霧立ちわたる
わが嘆く
息嘯の風に
霧立ちわたる

Over Mt. Ono
the mists ascend and hover—
driven by the sighs
I breathe in grief and sorrow,
the mists ascend and hover.

By Yamanoe Okura (d. 733?), one of the four major Manyo poets. His verse is distinguished by its subject matter, dealing in part with poverty, death, old age, and children; and by its philosophical cast, especially a strong Confucian strain, rare in this period, which doubtless was a result of his studies in China in 701. The above is an envoy to an elegy on the death of either his own or Tabito's wife (see following poem).
[5 : 799]

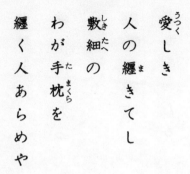

愛しき
人の纏きてし
敷細の
わが手枕を
纏く人あらめや

MY fair beloved
made a pillow of my arm
as she lay with me.
How could there be another
to make a pillow of it now!

*By Otomo Tabito (665-731), Yakamochi's father and
a great poet in his own right. His two series of verses
on the pleasures of wine and on the death of his wife
are highly valued.* [3 : 438]

琴取れば
なげき先立つ
けだしくも
琴の下樋に
嬬や匿れる

W HEN I take the harp,
all at once my grief breaks forth.
Could it be, perhaps,
that she, my true beloved,
hides within these very ribs?

*Apparently from the Kokashu. An elegy to the poet's
dead wife. The koto is often called a harp, a zither,
or a lute. Today it is about six feet long and seven
inches wide, with six strings running its length, and is
placed flat on the floor for playing; in Manyo times
it was much smaller and could be played on the lap.*

[7 : 1129]

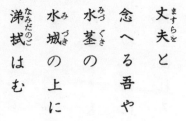

丈夫と
念へる吾や
水茎の
水城の上に
涕拭はむ

THOUGH I thought myself
till now a gallant warrior,
upon these ramparts
lying fresh at Mitsuki
I must wipe away my tears!

By Tabito. Written in 730 on the occasion of his departure from Dazaifu, the headquarters of the Kyushu defenses, where he had been in command for two years. The embankment at Mitsuki, where his departure ceremony presumably took place, had been thrown up to defend Dazaifu. This poem is a reply to verses by "a young woman named Kojima" lamenting his departure. [6 : 968]

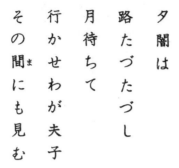

夕闇は
路たづたづし
月待ちて
行かせわが夫子
その間にも見む

IN twilight darkness
difficult would be your path:
await the moonrise,
and then go, that I may be
with you even that while more.

By "Okakeme, a young woman of Buzen." Buzen Province was in northern Kyushu and included Dazaifu. From internal evidence it has been surmised that this verse was written by a courtesan as part of her professional services. To the Japanese sensibility, the last line is particularly suspect, for its sensual selfishness. [4 : 709]

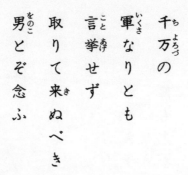

千万の
軍なりとも
言挙せず
取りて来ぬべき
男とぞ念ふ

THOUGH our foes may be
a million strong, I deem you
a gallant warrior
who will go without a word,
and return in victory.

*By Takahashi Mushimaro (early Nara period), a
representative poet of the early period who left many
ballad-like songs based on old legends. This is an envoy
to a poem commemorating the departure of Fujiwara
Umakai to eastern Kyushu on August 17, 732. The
painting shows a Gagaku court dancer in the role of
Ranryoō (Lan Ling-wang), a legendary warrior-prince
symbolizing martial victories.* [6 : 972]

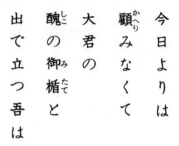

今日よりは
顧みなくて
大君の
醜の御楯と
出で立つ吾は

FROM this very day
without any homeward thoughts
I start my journey,
to become a lowly shield
of her mighty majesty.

By Imamatsuribe Yosofu, "a non-commissioned officer." This and the following seven poems are all from Volume 20 of the Manyoshu, *supposedly compiled by Yakamochi, and were composed in 754-55 by authors of the lowliest ranks among the military guard serving in the garrisons of the southern island of Kyushu. The anguish of partings and the uncertainties of military service become quite immediate in these verses.* [20 : 4373]

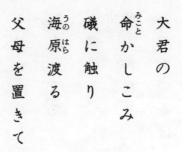

大君の
命かしこみ
（みこと）
磯に触り
海原渡る
（うのはら）
父母を置きて

IN awed obedience
to our majesty's command,
all along the coasts
I sail and cross the ocean,
leaving both my parents behind.

By Hasetsukabe Hitomaro, a frontier guard.

[20 : 4328]

88

父母が
頭かき撫で
幸くあれて
いひし言葉ぜ
忘れかねつる

THE words my father
and my mother spoke to me—
"We wish you luck, son"—
as they lightly stroked my head—
never can I forget them.

By Hasetsukabe Inamaro, a frontier guard.
[20 : 4346]

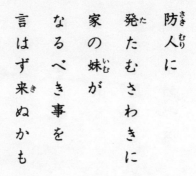

防人に
発たむさわきに
家の妹が
なるべき事を
言はず来ぬかも

IN the great to-do
at the time I started out
as a frontier guard,
of the things my wife should do
I said not a word—and left.

By Wakatoneribe Hirotari, a frontier guard.
[20 : 4364]

わが門の
片山椿
まこと汝れ
わが手触れなな
地に落ちもかも

HILLSIDE camellia,
you are blooming at my gate,
but you do not wish
my hand to touch your blossoms
for fear that they will scatter.

By Mononobe Hirotari, a frontier guard. Here a
heightened tenderness for all beautiful things expresses
the anguish of a soldier's parting.　　[20 : 4418]

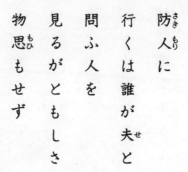

防人^{さきもり}に
行くは誰が夫^せと
問ふ人を
見るがともしさ
物思^{もひ}もせず

HOW I envy them
who ask indifferently
whose husband's going
to become a frontier guard,
not worrying in the least.

*Ascribed to an anonymous frontier guard but probably
by the guard's wife.* [20 : 4425]

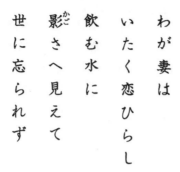

わが妻は
いたく恋ひらし
飲む水に
影（かご）さへ見えて
世に忘られず

Oh, my darling wife
must be longing much for me;
with her image clear
even on the water I drink,
I can never forget her.

By Wakayamatobe Mumaro, "a guard who was a district official." [20 : 4322]

小竹（さ）が葉の
さやく霜夜に
七（なな）重かる
衣（ころも）に益（ま）せる
子ろが膚（はだ）はも

WHEN nights are frosty
and the bamboo leaves stir cold,
though worn sevenfold,
all these robes are not so warm
as my beloved's body.

By an anonymous frontier guard. The original Japanese uses hada, *meaning "skin," "flesh," or "body." The painting further emphasizes this sensuous image by contrasting the wife's smooth complexion with the rough clay texture of a Haniwa grave figurine.*

[20 : 4431]

不尽の嶺に
零り置く雪は
六月の
十五日に消ぬれば
その夜降りけり

SHOULD the fallen snow
ever melt and fade away
from Mt. Fuji's peak
on the fifteenth day of June,
it would snow again that night.

*From the "Mushimaro Collection" (early Nara period),
author unknown. One of two envoys to a longer poem
on Mt. Fuji. Then as now the majestic Mt. Fuji domi-
nated the Kanto "Eastland" both topographically and
symbolically.* [3 : 320]

95

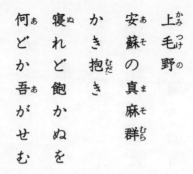

上毛野の
安蘇の真麻群
かき抱き
寝れど飽かぬを
何どか吾がせむ

Aᴛ Kamitsuke,
bundling the hemp of Aso
tightly in my arms,
I never tire of bundling:
what am I to do with you?

Anonymous Azuma-uta. The first three lines are a most skillful use of the joshi device (see p. 75), pivoting on the word "bundle," used to apply both to the hemp and the girl; whereas the earlier use was largely on a verbal level, here it contributes to the whole air of the poem. [14 : 3404]

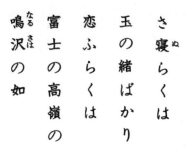

さ寝らくは
玉の緒ばかり
恋ふらくは
富士の高嶺の
鳴沢の如

OH, sleeping with you
lasts only for a moment;
but longing for you
is like the roaring rapids
rushing down from Fuji's peak.

Anonymous Azuma-uta.   [14 : 3358]

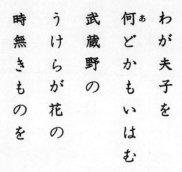

わが夫子を
何ぞかもいはむ
武蔵野の
うけらが花の
時無きものを

OF the one I love,
in all truth what shall I say?
On Musashi Plain
the wild ovata blossoms
are all blowing, timelessly.

Anonymous Azuma-uta. The Atractylis ovata *is a
thistle-like wildflower that blooms throughout the summer; here the poetess's thoughts, like the flower's long
blooming, are ever of her lover.* [14 : 3379]

筑波嶺の
新桑繭の
衣はあれど
君が御衣し
あやに著欲しも

ALTHOUGH I have silks
new-made from cocoons that fed
on mulberry leaves
gathered on Mt. Tsukuba,
how I wish to try yours on!

*Anonymous Azuma-uta. Clothes were exchanged by
bride and groom at the marriage ceremony.*

[14:3350]

児毛知山
若鶏冠木の
もみつまで
寝も と吾は思ふ
汝は何どか思ふ

Until young maples
turn to gold and crimson-red
on Mt. Komochi,
would that I could lie with you—
won't you come and lie with me?

Anonymous Azuma-uta. The question in the last line suggests the utagaki (song-fence) ceremony, in which young men and women formed two lines facing each other and tossed poems or songs back and forth as a form of courtship. The name of the mountain can also be read as "child-holding" or "pregnancy."

[14 : 3494]

足柄の
箱根の嶺ろの
和草の
花つ妻なれや
紐解かず寝む

LIKE the maidenhair
blooming on Hakone Peak
at Ashigari,
she is fair indeed, and yet
with her cords tied fast she sleeps.

*Anonymous Azuma-uta. Of the many interpretations
of this obscure verse, that followed here has it that a
lusty young lover is taunting his sweetheart with being
beautiful to look at but useless as a doll. "To untie
one's cords" is a euphemism for making love, and the
negative figure here probably also derives from the
tightly curled buds of the maidenhair fern. The preen-
ing bird of the painting might stand for either the
impatient lover or, in the sense of fine feathers not
always making fine birds, the reluctant maiden.*

[14 : 3370]

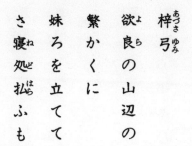

梓弓^{あづさゆみ}
欲良^{よら}の山辺の
繁かくに
妹ろを立てて
さ寝^ね処^ど払^{はら}ふも

BESIDE the thicket
at the foot of Yora Hill
I kept her standing
while I tidied up the spot
where we would lie together.

*Anonymous Azuma-uta. Perhaps this verse also was
sung at an ütagaki (see p. 100) or describes a success-
ful aftermath.* [14 : 3489]

葛飾の
真間の手古名を
まことかも
吾に寄すとふ
真間の手児名を

Is it really true
fair Tekona of Mama
in Katsushika
will be chosen as my bride?
Fair Tekona of Mama . . .

Anonymous Azuma-uta. Tekona the Fair appears in several poems, but little is known of her except that she was surpassingly beautiful, died by drowning, and was a commoner. Mama was a village in a district that now forms part of Tokyo. The repetition in the second and fifth lines is a classic folk-song pattern.
[14 : 3384]

麻苧ら^{あさを}を
麻笥^{をけ}に多^{ふすさ}に
績^うまずとも
明日^{あす}著^きせさめや
いざせ小床^{をどこ}に

EVEN though you spin
the pail full of hempen thread,
by tomorrow's light
you can hardly wear new cloth.
Oh, come into my small bed!

Anonymous Azuma-uta. Hemp cloth was widely used among commoners. [14 : 3484]

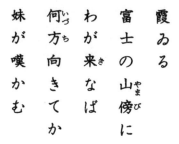

霞ゐる
富士の山傍に
わが来なば
何方向きてか
妹が嘆かむ

IF I go from her,
far away to Mt. Fuji
where the mists arise,
which way, in what direction,
can she turn to long for me?

Anonymous Azuma-uta.   [14 : 3357]

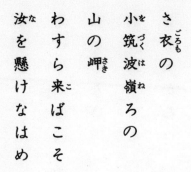

さ衣の
小筑波嶺ろの
山の岬に
わすら来ばこそ
汝を懸けなはめ

As you journey on
beyond the lofty summit
of Mt. Tsukuba,
if you should forget me then,
I will never speak to you.

Anonymous Azuma-uta.   [14 : 3394]

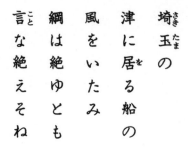

埼<ruby>玉<rt>たま</rt></ruby>の<ruby>津<rt>さき</rt></ruby>に<ruby>居<rt>を</rt></ruby>る船の風をいたみ綱は絶ゆとも<ruby>言<rt>こと</rt></ruby>な絶えそね

EVEN if your ship
in Sakitama Harbor
find the wind too strong
and its ropes be snapped off short,
do not ever break your word.

Anonymous Azuma-uta.   [14 : 3380]

107

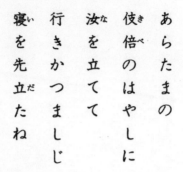

あらたまの
伎倍^きのはやしに
汝^なを立てて
行きかつましじ
寝^いを先立^だたね

LEAVING you to stand
there beside the grove of trees
at Kibe, my love,
I cannot start my journey:
first I'd like to sleep with you.

Anonymous Azuma-uta. This poem presents several difficulties in reading and interpretation. [14: 3353]

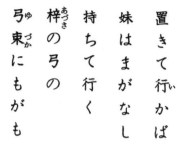

置きて行かば
妹はまがなし
持ちて行く
梓（あづさ）の弓の
弓束（ゆづか）にもがも

How will you bear it
when I leave you home and go?
If only you were
the grip of the birchwood bow
I shall carry in my hand!

Azuma-uta, by an anonymous frontier guard. Note the characteristic mode of expression: it would be unmanly and selfish, from the Japanese point of view, for the soldier to dwell on his own anguish at parting from his wife. Rather, he expresses his concern for his wife's loneliness. [14 : 3567]

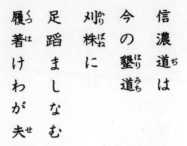

信濃道は
今の墾道に
刈株に
足踏ましなむ
履著けわが夫

NOW newly opened
is the way to Shinano:
oh, do not stumble
over the stumps in the road;
wear your good straw boots, my love.

Anonymous Azuma-uta. This is the only Azuma-uta that can be dated with any accuracy, since the road to Shinano was completed in June, 713. [14 : 3399]

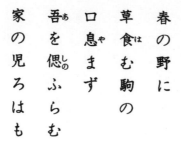

春の野に
草食む駒の
口息まず
吾を偲ふらむ
家の児ろはも

IN the spring meadow
the mare that feeds on grasses
never stops eating;
so my love who stays at home
never stops longing for me.

Anonymous Azuma-uta. A verse written during a journey. [14 : 3532]

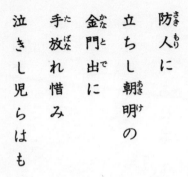

OH, the dawn I left
to become a frontier guard,
by our cottage gate
how she wept, my loving wife,
unwilling to free my hand!

Azuma-uta by an anonymous frontier guard.
[14 : 3569]

青楊の
萌らろ川門に
汝を待つと
清水は汲まず
立処ならすも

AT the river-ford
where grow the bud-green willows,
waiting long for you. . . .
Instead of drawing water
I smooth the spot I stand on.

Anonymous Azuma-uta. This is considered a good poem because of the aptness of the description of the waiting girl's actions. Idly she pats and smooths the ground with her foot, whiling away the tedium of waiting. [14 : 3546]

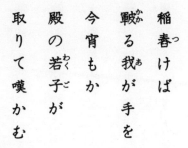

稲春っけば
鞁る我が手を
今宵もか
殿の若子が
取りて嘆かむ

EVEN though my hands
are rough from much rice-pounding,
on this night again
my master's son will clasp them
with a heavy, broken sigh.

Anonymous Azuma-uta. Possibly a tanka version of a work-song for group singing. Rice was polished by pounding it in a mortar with a large mallet.

[14 : 3459]

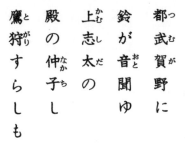

都武賀野に
鈴が音聞ゆ
上志太の
殿の仲子し
鷹狩すらしも

THE bells are tinkling
across Tsumuga Meadows.
The younger lordling
of Kamushida Manor
must be hawking in the fields.

*Anonymous Azuma-uta. The bells are those attached
to the hawks.* [14 : 3438]

おもしろき
野をばな焼きそ
古草に
新草まじり
生ひば生ふるがに

OH, do not set fire
to such a lovely meadow:
with the old grey grass
the new will grow and mingle.
Let it burgeon as it will!

Anonymous Azuma-uta. Although labeled an Azuma-uta, the delicacy of the sentiment and refinement of rhythm would suggest that it might have been written by a sophisticated townsman or courtier in imitation of a rustic "song of the Eastland." [14 : 3452]

INDEX OF FIRST LINES

INDEX OF AUTHORS AND OTHER ITEMS

Page numbers in italics indicate poems
by the person or in the category named.

Other TUT BOOKS

JAPANESE THINGS: Being Notes on Various Subjects Connected with Japan *by Basil Hall Chamberlain*

KAPPA *by Ryūnosuke Akutagawa; translated by Geoffrey Bownas*

KOKORO: Hints and Echoes of Japanese Inner Life *by Lafcadio Hearn*

KWAIDAN: Stories and Studies of Strange Things *by Lafcadio Hearn*

THE LIFE OF BUDDHA *by A. Ferdinand Herold*

NIHONGI: Chronicles of Japan from the Earliest Times to A.D. **697** *by W. G. Aston*

SHADOWINGS *by Lafcadio Hearn*

THE TEN FOOT SQUARE HUT AND TALES OF THE HEIKE: Being Two Thirteenth-century Japanese classics, the "Hojoki" and selections from the "Heike Monogatari" *translated by A. L. Sadler*

TO LIVE IN JAPAN *by Mary Lee O'Neal and Virginia Woodruff*

CHARLES E. TUTTLE CO., INC.

Please order from your bookstore or write directly to:

or:

Suido 1-chome, 2–6, Bunkyo-ku, Tokyo

Rutland, Vermont 05701 U.S.A.